Crafts for Kids Who Are
LEARNING ABOUT
WEATHER

Crafts for Kids Who Are
LEARNING ABOUT
WEATHER

KATHY ROSS
Illustrated by Jan Barger

M Millbrook Press   Minneapolis

To Kodi, my friend who is sunny no matter what the weather!

Millbrook Press
A division of Lerner Publishing Group
241 First Avenue North
Minneapolis, Minnesota 55401 U.S.A.

Website address: www.lernerbooks.com

Library of Congress Cataloging-in-Publication Data

Ross, Kathy (Katharine Reynolds), 1948–
     Crafts for kids who are learning about— weather / by Kathy Ross ;
 illustrations by Jan Barger.
        p.   cm. — (Crafts for kids who are learning about—)
     ISBN-13: 978–0–7613–2796–7 (lib. bdg. : alk. paper)
     ISBN-10: 0–7613–2796–7 (lib. bdg. : alk. paper)
     1. Weather—Study and teaching (Elementary)—Activity pro-
 grams—Juvenile literature. 2. Weather—Experiments—Juvenile literature. 3. Activity programs in education—Juvenile literature. I.
 Title: Weather. II. Barger, Jan, 1948- ill. III. Title.
 QC981.3.R65 2006
 372.35—dc22   2004030764

Manufactured in the United States of America
1 2 3 4 5 6 – JR – 11 10 09 08 07 06

Table of Contents

What Kind of Weather? Wheel

Here is what you need:

two uncoated white
paper plates

markers

scissors

paper fastener

LOOK OUT YOUR
WINDOW AND SEE
WHAT KIND OF
WEATHER YOU ARE
HAVING TODAY.

Here is what you do:

1. Draw a light line down the center of the eating side of one paper plate. Draw another line across the center of the plate so that the plate is divided into four equal parts.

2. Use a marker to draw a window outline in one quadrant of the eating side of the second paper plate.

3. Use the scissors to cut the window shape out of the plate.

4. Use the markers to add the wall and floor plus whatever other details you would like your room to have.

5. Set the plate with the window on top of the other plate.

6. Poke the fastener through the center of the two plates. Bend the arms of the fastener out to each side to secure the two plates together.

7. Turn the back plate around a few times until it is turning smoothly on the fastener.

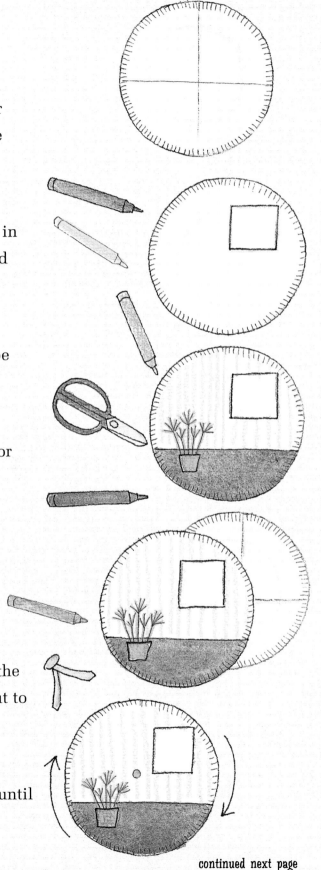

continued next page

8. Center one of the quartered-off sections of the back plate so that it is visible through the window.

9. Draw a scene outside the window as it would look in sunny weather.

10. Turn the plate so that the sunny scene is hidden and the next quarter of the plate shows through the cut window.

11. On this section draw the exact same scene out the window as it would look in windy weather.

12. Continue turning the plate, drawing the same scene in rainy weather and, finally, in snowy weather.

You might want to use collage materials to decorate your room with a window. You could cut a pet cat or dog and some pictures for the wall from magazines. Try fabric scraps for the curtains and a table made from toothpicks. I'm sure you'll have your own ideas for decorating.

What kind of weather is outside your window today?

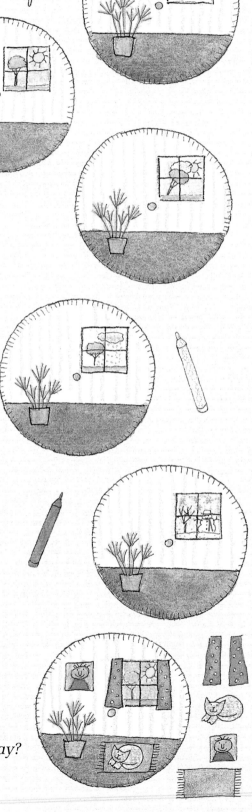

Dress for the Weather Doll

Here is what you need:

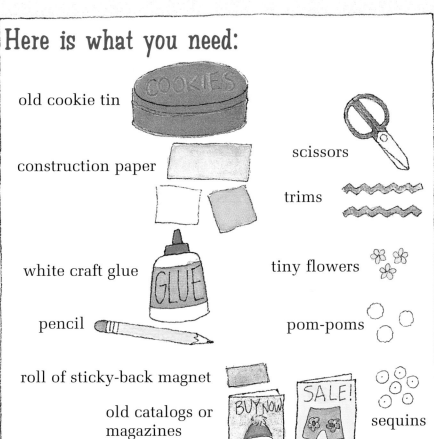

old cookie tin

construction paper

scissors

trims

white craft glue

tiny flowers

pencil

pom-poms

roll of sticky-back magnet

old catalogs or magazines

sequins

Here is what you do:

1. Trace around the lid of the tin on white paper. Cut around the inside of the traced line to get a piece of paper that fits inside the lid of the tin. Use this circle as a pattern for making different scenery to fit inside the lid.

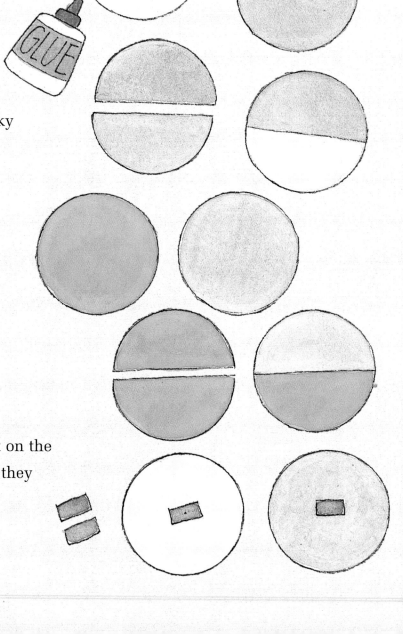

2. For winter cut a white and a blue circle. Cut the blue circle in half and glue one half of it over the top of the white circle to look like sky above the snow.

3. Cut a green and a blue circle to make a scene to use in summer, fall, and spring.

4. Put pieces of sticky-back magnet on the back of the scenes you make so that they will stick to the lid of the tin.

5. Make details to add to the scenes for different seasons. Whatever you make or use will need a small piece of sticky-back magnet on the back to attach it to the scene. You can make things from paper or use things like snowflake-shaped sequins, tiny artificial flowers, pom-pom snowballs, animal pictures, trees, and whatever else you might think of.

6. Finally, you will need a person to stand in your scene. You can draw your own or purchase one in the scrapbook section of your favorite craft store. If you purchase one, it will probably come with some clothes to get you started. Otherwise, over time, make the doll paper outfits for all different kinds of weather. You might also find some things the doll can use in old catalogs and magazines. That would be a good place to find an umbrella or some snow boots and some neat hats. Remember that everything you make or use will need a piece of sticky-back magnet on the back to attach it to the tin.

This is a project that you can add to over time. Store all the pieces you make in the base of the tin and set up different scenes in the lid.

Mr. Thermometer

A THERMOMETER IS USED TO TELL US HOW HOT OR COLD IT IS.

Here is what you need:

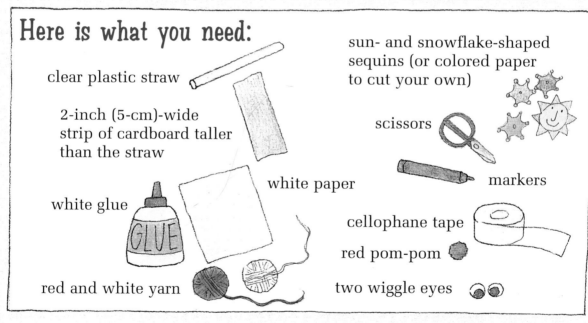

clear plastic straw

2-inch (5-cm)-wide strip of cardboard taller than the straw

white glue

white paper

red and white yarn

sun- and snowflake-shaped sequins (or colored paper to cut your own)

scissors

markers

cellophane tape

red pom-pom

two wiggle eyes

Here is what you do:

1. Cover the cardboard by wrapping it in white paper to make it look like the back of a thermometer.

2. If you are using a flexi-straw, cut off the flexi part.

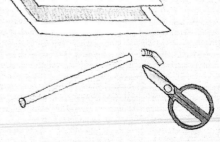

3. Cut a red piece of yarn and a white piece of yarn that are both about 4 inches (10 cm) longer than the height of the cardboard.

4. Tie the ends of the two pieces of yarn together.

5. Thread the end of the red yarn through the straw by pushing it in the straw and then sucking on the other end to bring it through.

6. Tie the ends of the red and the white yarn together to make a loop through the straw.

7. Tape the straw to the center of the cardboard with the loop behind the cardboard.

8. Glue the wiggle eyes on each side of the straw and the red pom-pom on the straw below the eyes for a nose.

9. Glue a sun near the top of the thermometer and a snowflake near the bottom.

10. You can copy some of the numbers from a real thermometer on your thermometer puppet if you want to.

When it is cold, the red line of mercury on the thermometer is down low, and when it is hot, the red moves up higher on the thermometer. Pull on the loop of yarn from behind to make the red line on Mr. Thermometer move up or down.

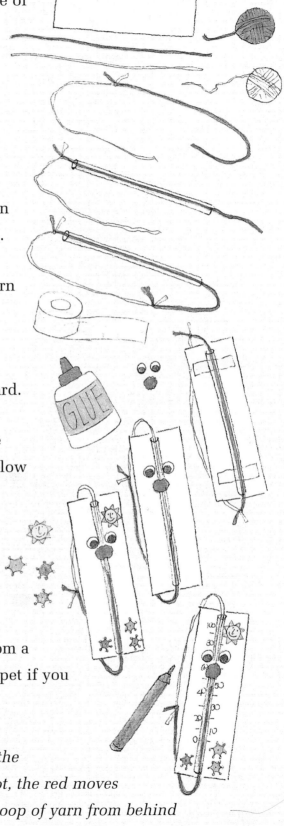

13

Huffing, Puffing Wind Tissue Box

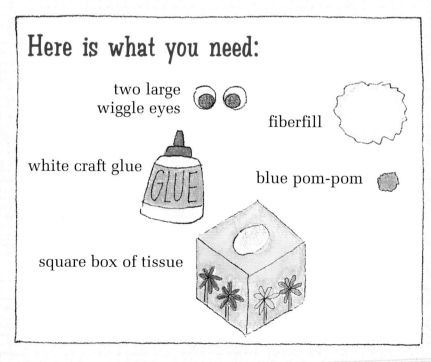

Here is what you need:

two large wiggle eyes

fiberfill

white craft glue

GLUE

blue pom-pom

square box of tissue

MOVING AIR IS CALLED WIND.

Here is what you do:

1. Glue fiberfill around the opening of the tissue box to represent the wind.

2. Glue the two wiggle eyes above the opening in the tissue box.

3. Glue the blue pom-pom below the eyes, but above the opening, for the nose.

4. Turn the box of tissue on one side with the eyes and nose above the opening. Pull the first tissue partway out of the box to look like the wind is huffing and puffing.

*Whoooooooooooo . . . !
Can you hear the wind?*

Mr. Wind Puppet

Here is what you need:

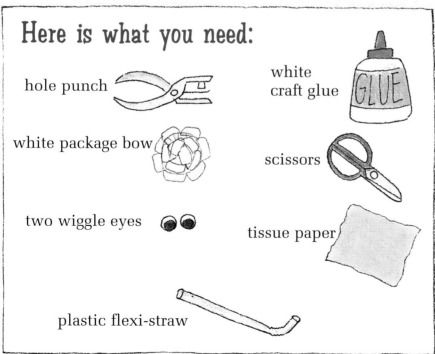

hole punch

white package bow

two wiggle eyes

plastic flexi-straw

white craft glue

scissors

tissue paper

SOMETIMES THE WIND WILL BLOW DRY LEAVES AND OTHER THINGS AROUND.

Here is what you do:

1. Punch a hole through one side of the bottom cardboard of the bow and about two layers of bow. You may need to do each punch separately.

2. Slide the bent end of the flexi-straw through the holes so that it sticks out slightly from one side of the bow for a mouth.

3. Glue the two wiggle eyes to the bow above the mouth.

4. Cut some 1-inch (2.5-cm) leaves from tissue paper.

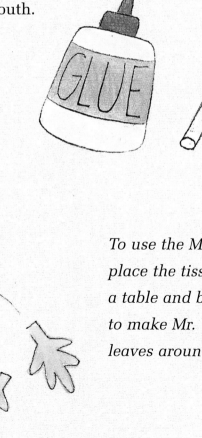

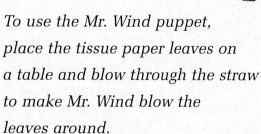

To use the Mr. Wind puppet, place the tissue paper leaves on a table and blow through the straw to make Mr. Wind blow the leaves around.

17

Wind Bells

Here is what you need:

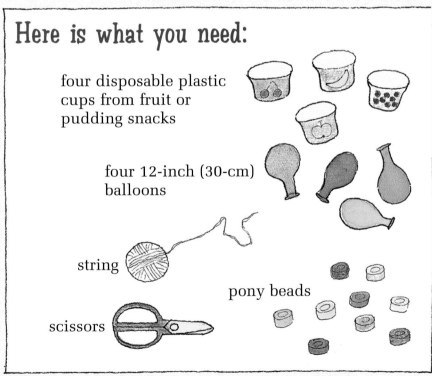

four disposable plastic
cups from fruit or
pudding snacks

four 12-inch (30-cm)
balloons

string

pony beads

scissors

HANG THIS
PROJECT OUTSIDE
AND LET THE WIND
MAKE MUSIC.

Here is what you do:

1. Cut off the neck of each of the balloons.

2. To make each of the four bells, poke a small hole in the bottom of a snack cup.

3. Thread a 16-inch (40-cm) length of string through the hole from the bottom to the inside of the cup. Tie a bead to the end to keep the end of the string inside the cup from coming back through the hole.

4. Drop a few pony beads into the cup.

5. Cover the cup with a balloon, pulling the balloon tight across the opening of the cup and up over it.

6. Thread several pony beads onto the string of each bell.

7. Tie the ends of the strings of the four bells together about 6 inches (15 cm) from the top.

8. Thread some pony beads over all four strings, then knot the strings again just above the beads.

9. Tie the ends of the strings together to make a loop for hanging the bells.

Find a breezy spot to hang the wind bells and listen to the gentle rattle.

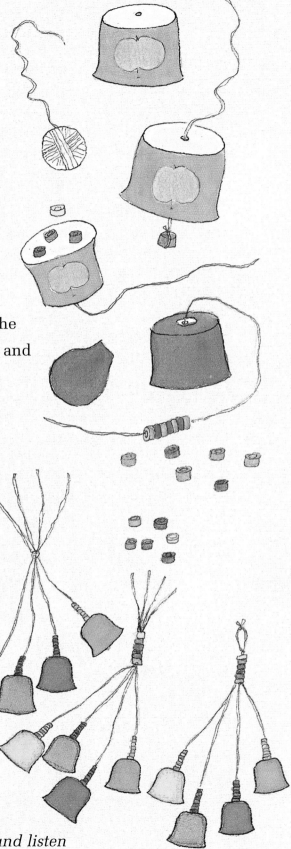

Sun Behind a Cloud

Here is what you need:

sliding matchbox

markers

fiberfill

white pom-pom

white craft glue   GLUE

two wiggle eyes

THE EARTH GETS WARMTH FROM THE SUN.

Here is what you do:

1. Slide the inner box out of the matchbox.

2. Use the markers to draw a picture of the sun in the sky on the bottom of the inner box.

3. Glue a puff of fiberfill over the top of the outer box to look like a cloud.

4. Glue the two wiggle eyes on the cloud.

5. Glue the white pom-pom below the eyes for a nose.

6. Slide the end of the box back into the outer box so that the sun is visible next to the cloud.

7. Close the box to hide the sun behind the cloud.

Have you ever noticed that when the sun goes behind a cloud, it feels cooler and seems darker?

21

Sun Puppet and Disappearing Puddle

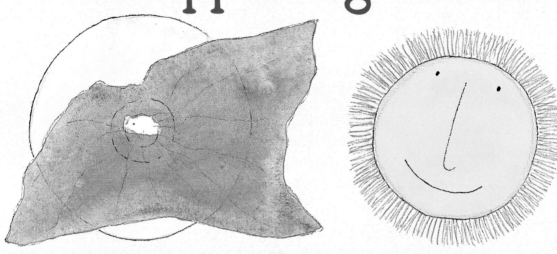

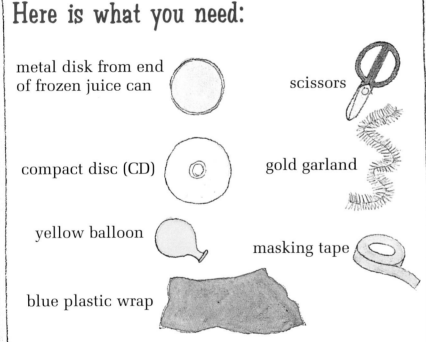

Here is what you need:

metal disk from end of frozen juice can

compact disc (CD)

yellow balloon

blue plastic wrap

scissors

gold garland

masking tape

THE SUN DRIES UP PUDDLES OF WATER AFTER IT RAINS.

Here is what you do:

1. Cut off the neck of the balloon.

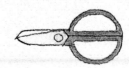

2. Cover the disc with the balloon to become the sun, keeping the balloon opening near the edge of the disc.

3. Cut a piece of gold garland long enough to go around the outside of the sun.

4. Use masking tape to tape the garland around the edge of one side of the sun. This will be the back of the project.

5. Tear off a square of blue plastic wrap to use as water for the puddle.

6. Push the center of the wrap down through the hole on the silver side of the CD.

7. To use the sun puppet, slide your finger between the opening in the balloon and the metal disc. Shine the sun on the puddle. Holding the puddle by the center of the plastic wrap underneath, keep pulling the plastic wrap through the hole in the CD, making it look smaller and smaller until the puddle disappears.

The water from a puddle really goes up in the air when a puddle disappears, forming clouds.

Rain
in a
Bag

Here is what you need:

two zip-to-close
plastic bags

fiberfill

permanent markers

blue and/or
silver glitter

CLOUDS MADE OF
WATER DROPLETS
BECOME SO HEAVY
THE WATER FALLS
TO EARTH AS RAIN.

Here is what you do:

1. Turn one of the zip-to-close bags inside out. You should now be able to attach it to the second bag by zipping the sides of the two bags together. Try it.

2. Place a handful of fiberfill in one of the bags for clouds.

3. Use the permanent markers to draw an outdoor scene on the bottom of one side of the second bag.

4. Place about a teaspoon of glitter inside the bag with the scene drawn on it.

5. Zip the two bags together so that the bag with the cloud is above the bag with the outdoor scene.

6. Turn the bags upside down so that the glitter goes up and sticks to the fiberfill clouds in the top bag.

7. Turn the bags right-side-up and shake gently to make the rain fall from the cloud.

To make it rain harder, add more glitter "rain" to your bag.

Teeny, Tiny Muddy Footprints

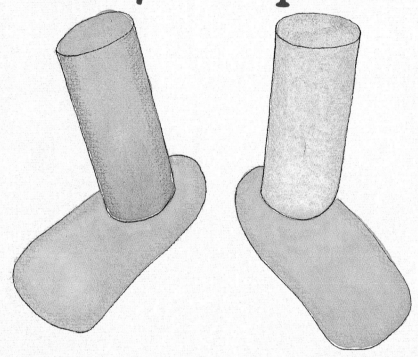

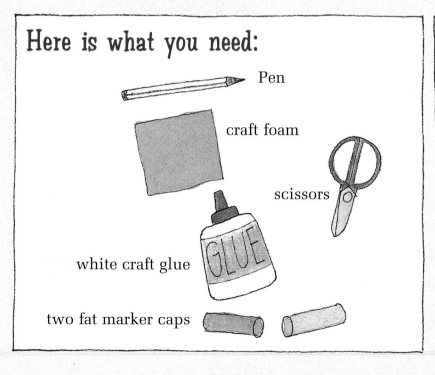

Here is what you need:

Pen

craft foam

scissors

white craft glue

two fat marker caps

RAINY DAYS MEAN MUD PUDDLES.

Here is what you do:

1. Use the pen to draw two 2-inch (5-cm)-long foot shapes, a right one and a left one, on the craft foam.

2. Cut out the two foot shapes.

3. Glue the closed end of a marker cap to the center of each foot shape. Let the glue dry completely.

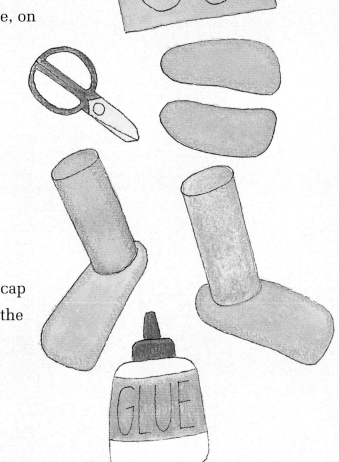

To have some fun with the teeny, tiny foot shapes, slip a marker cap on your index and middle fingers. Now go outside after a rainstorm and find some mud to walk the tiny foot shapes through. Next, walk them on a sidewalk to leave some mysterious little footprints for others to wonder about. How silly!

Rainbow Flower Garden Stake

Here is what you need:

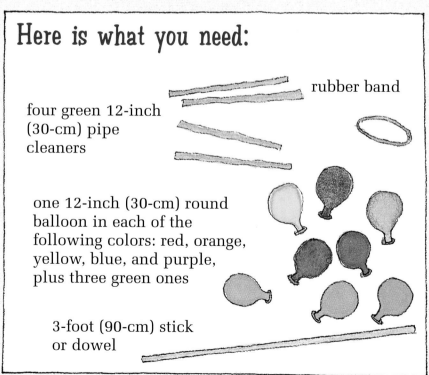

rubber band

four green 12-inch (30-cm) pipe cleaners

one 12-inch (30-cm) round balloon in each of the following colors: red, orange, yellow, blue, and purple, plus three green ones

3-foot (90-cm) stick or dowel

SOMETIMES WHEN THE SUN SHINES THROUGH THE RAIN, YOU CAN SEE A COLORFUL RAINBOW.

Here is what you do:

1. Bend the four pipe cleaners in half.

2. Slide one end of each of three pipe cleaners into a different color balloon.

3. Use the rubber band to attach the folded ends of the pipe cleaners to one end of the stick or dowel.

4. Spread the balloons around the top to look like the petals of a flower.

5. Wrap any excess pipe cleaner around the base of the flower.

6. Slide the two green balloons over the ends of the last pipe cleaner.

7. Wrap the center part of the pipe cleaner around the stick about 6 inches (15 cm) below the flower to secure the balloons to the stick to form the leaves.

Push the end of the flower into the dirt in your yard or garden and enjoy the rainbow of pretty colors. You might want to "plant" more than one!

Flash of Lightning Puppet

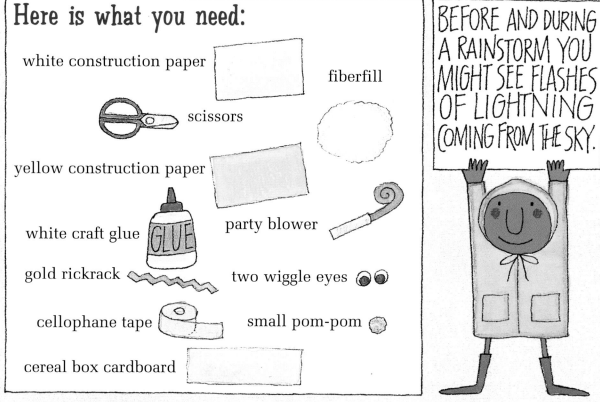

Here is what you need:

white construction paper

scissors

fiberfill

yellow construction paper

white craft glue GLUE

party blower

gold rickrack

two wiggle eyes

cellophane tape

small pom-pom

cereal box cardboard

Here is what you do:

1. Hold the white construction paper on top of the cardboard and cut out a cloud shape that will cover the party blower.

2. Cut a yellow construction paper zigzag of lightning that is as long as the party blower when it is stretched out.

3. Tape the two ends of the lightning to the stretched-out party blower, then allow the lightning to curl back into the blower.

4. Cut a slit in the top of one side of the cloud.

5. Slip the mouthpiece of the party blower through the slit so that the mouthpiece is behind the cloud at the top.

6. Use tape to secure the party blower to the front of the cloud.

7. Glue the two sides of the back of the cloud to the cardboard. Cut a small piece out at the top of the cardboard so that you can blow on the mouthpiece of the party blower.

8. Glue fiberfill over the front of the cloud to cover it and the top part of the party blower.

9. Stretch the fiberfill over the curled part of the party blower to hide it. Do not glue it to this part or the party blower will no longer stretch open when blown.

10. Give the cloud a face by gluing on the two wiggle eyes, a pom-pom nose, and a strip of rickrack for the mouth.

To make a streak of lightning flash from the cloud, then disappear, blow on the mouthpiece of the party blower.

Thunder Cloud Puppet

WHEN YOU SEE LIGHTNING, YOU WILL OFTEN HEAR THUNDER A FEW SECONDS LATER.

Here is what you need:

9-inch by 12-inch (23- by 30-cm) sheet of white construction paper

two 12-inch (30-cm) gold sparkle stems

empty toothpaste box

scissors

stapler

black construction paper scrap

white craft glue

fiberfill

12-inch (30-cm) black pipe cleaner

few pony beads or old buttons

Here is what you do:

1. Drop a few beads or buttons into the toothpaste box. Close the open end of the box and secure it with glue.

2. Fold a sheet of white construction paper over the toothpaste box to cover it on both sides.

3. Staple the sides of the paper together just below and on each side of the toothpaste box.

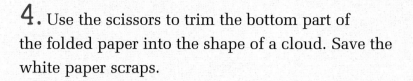

4. Use the scissors to trim the bottom part of the folded paper into the shape of a cloud. Save the white paper scraps.

5. Fold the two gold sparkle stems into zigzags to look like lightning.

6. Staple the end of each pipe cleaner between the two sides of the cloud and coming out from the bottom.

7. Staple around the edges of the cloud to hold the front and back paper together.

8. Glue fiberfill over both sides of the cloud.

9. Cut eyes for the cloud from the black and white construction paper scraps.

10. Glue the eyes to the top part of one side of the cloud.

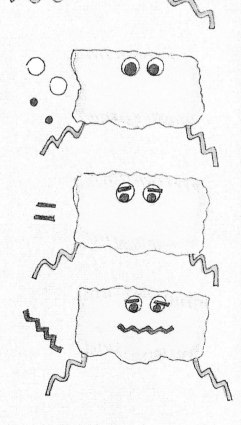

11. Cut two pieces from the black pipe cleaner to use as eyebrows. Glue the brows across the top part of the eyes.

12. Bend the remaining piece of black pipe cleaner into a zigzag and glue it on the cloud below the eyes for a mouth.

13. Shake the cloud to hear the thunder rumble.

Use the Thunder Cloud Puppet with the Flash of Lightning Puppet to create a thunderstorm of your own!

Pretty Spring Umbrella

WHEN IT RAINS, PEOPLE WILL OFTEN CARRY AN UMBRELLA TO KEEP FROM GETTING WET.

Here is what you need:

white craft glue

scissors

pretty ribbon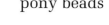

12-inch (30-cm) pipe cleaner

pretty-color tissue paper

old party hat

empty thin craft ribbon spool

ruffle lace or other trim

pony beads

Here is what you do:

1. Thread a 12-inch (30-cm) pipe cleaner through the top inside of the hat so that it pokes out the top about an inch. Secure the pipe cleaner in place with a dab of glue.

2. Cut a circle of tissue paper large enough to completely cover the outside of the party hat.

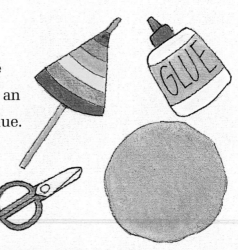

3. Cover the outside of the party hat with glue, then smooth the paper over the gluey hat to cover it. You will need to poke the pipe cleaner tip through the paper at the center to bring it down around the hat. Try to smooth the paper down so that it pleats evenly like a real folded umbrella would.

4. Trim the excess tissue paper from around the edge of the umbrella.

5. Glue pretty ruffle lace or other trim around the edge of the umbrella.

6. Slide a pony bead over the end of the pipe cleaner at the tip of the umbrella and glue it in place.

7. Peel one end off the cardboard ribbon spool.

8. Thread the pipe cleaner through the hole in the spool and push the cardboard down into the umbrella
as far as it will go. Secure the edges with glue. This will keep the pipe cleaner umbrella handle centered inside the umbrella.

9. Fold the end of the pipe cleaner handle into a curve. Slide a few beads on the handle and secure with glue to decorate.

10. Tie a bow around the handle.

One or more of these umbrellas look great hung from the ceiling by a ribbon tied to the handle. You can also use them as party favors. Just put ca ndy or small prizes inside each hat before putting the ribbon spool support inside.

So Cold I
Can See
My Breath!
Plate Face

Here is what you need:

three uncoated white paper plates

white craft glue

old colored adult-size sock with stretchy cuff

fiberfill

thin craft ribbon

scissors

stapler

markers

WHEN THE TEMPERATURE DROPS BELOW FREEZING YOU CAN ACTUALLY SEE YOUR OWN BREATH.

Here is what you do:

1. Stack the three plates on top of each other, then glue them together around the edges. This will make the project sturdier than if you used just one paper plate.

2. Use the markers to draw hair, eyes, and a nose on the eating side of the top plate.

3. Cut an X shape where the mouth should be.

4. Use the markers to draw a round mouth around the cut so that it looks like the mouth of a person blowing.

5. Rub some glue on the cut in the mouth. Stuff a small amount of fiberfill into the cut to look like breath coming out of the mouth.

6. Cut the cuff from the sock.

7. Tie one end of the cuff closed with a piece of ribbon. Tie the ribbon in a bow.

8. Stretch the open end of the cuff over the top part of the head to look like a hat. Staple the hat in place on each side of the head.

Do you live where it gets cold enough to see your breath?

Icy Snowman Mobile

Here is what you need:

three plastic disposable tubs, one slightly larger than the others

water

heavy string or thin rope

fabric scrap

large dark-colored buttons

scissors

carrot

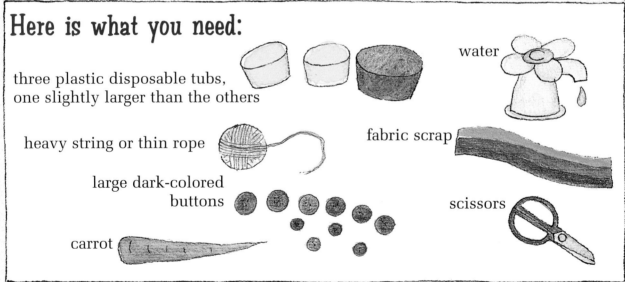

Here is what you do:

1. You will need to do this project on a flat surface, outside, on a day when the temperature is below freezing.

2. Line the three plastic tubs up like a snowman, putting the larger tub at the bottom of the snowman.

3. Now arrange the tubs so that there is about 2 inches (5 cm) of space between each section of the snowman.

4. Set a piece of rope or heavy string across the center of the three tubs, pushing the rope down into each of the tubs. Tie the top end of the rope into a loop to use for hanging the finished snowman. Trim off any excess rope.

5. Arrange the buttons in the bottom of the top tub to represent eyes and a smile for the snowman.

6. Add a carrot sticking out of one side of the tub for the nose.

7. Add buttons to the center tub for the buttons on the belly of the snowman.

8. Carefully fill each container with water.

9. Leave the project outdoors overnight to freeze. In the morning pop the snowman out of the molds.

10. Tie the fabric scrap around his neck for a scarf, and hang your snowman mobile up outside.

You can also do this project inside on a tray, then carry the tray with the assembled project outside to freeze.

WHEN THE TEMPERATURE DROPS BELOW FREEZING, RAIN BECOMES SNOW AND YOU CAN GO OUTSIDE AND BUILD A SNOWMAN!

Changing Face Snowman

Here is what you need:

three identical empty white spools from thread

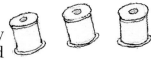

scissors

rickrack trim

felt scrap

white craft glue

permanent markers

old stretchy knit glove

12-inch (30-cm) white pipe cleaner

Here is what you do:

1. Thread the three spools onto the white pipe cleaner so that about 1 inch (2.5 cm) of the pipe cleaner sticks out from the top of the stack of spools.

2. Glue the bottom two spools together, but do not glue the top spool to the middle spool.

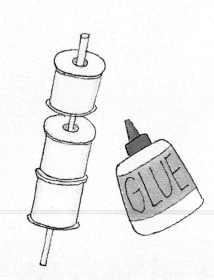

3. Cut the thumb from the old glove to make a hat for the snowman.

4. Thread the top end of the pipe cleaner inside and through the top of the hat. Slide the hat down the pipe cleaner and pull the ends over the top spool to look like a hat.

5. Fold the end of the pipe cleaner down, thread it back into the hat, and squeeze it to secure the pipe cleaner to the top of the hat.

6. Glue some rickrack or other trim around the rim of the hat to decorate it.

7. Tie a scrap of felt around the top of the second spool for a scarf. Use scissors to cut fringe on the two ends of the scarf. Secure the scarf to the snowman with some glue.

8. Use a marker to draw some buttons on the center spool of the snowman.

9. Bend the bottom piece of pipe cleaner to one side.

10. Trim the bottom piece of pipe cleaner so it is about 3 inches (8 cm) long.

11. Use the markers to draw three different faces for the snowman on the top spool. Make the three faces equal distances apart around the spool head.

12. To change the face on the snowman turn the head using the pipe cleaner at the bottom as a handle.

You might want to use collage materials such as sequins and cut paper when creating the three different faces for the snowman.

Snow Shovel Magnet

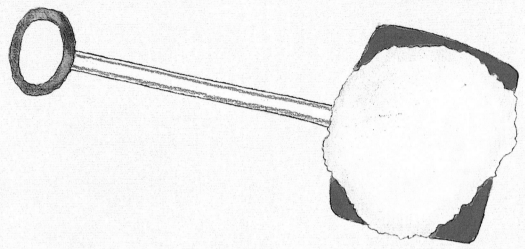

Here is what you need:

red disposable plastic plate

ruler

white craft glue

GLUE

scissors

fiberfill

plastic straw

pipe cleaner

piece of sticky-back magnet

WHEN IT SNOWS, PEOPLE USE A SHOVEL TO CLEAR THE SNOW FROM WALKWAYS.

Here is what you do:

1. Cut a 1 1/2-inch by 2-inch (3.75- by 5-cm) piece from the plastic plate for the shovel scoop.

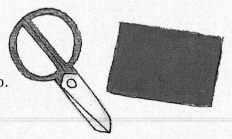

2. Trim around the piece, rounding the corners.

3. Cut a 3-inch (8-cm) piece of plastic straw for the handle of the shovel.

4. Cut a small slit through one end of the straw. Slide the center of the long end of the shovel scoop into the slit. Secure the handle to the shovel scoop with glue.

5. Dip one end of the pipe cleaner in glue. Slide the gluey end of the pipe cleaner into the straw handle of the shovel. Trim the other end of the pipe cleaner so that about 2 inches (5 cm) sticks out of the end of the straw.

6. Bend the end of the pipe cleaner to form a handle for the shovel.

7. Glue a small amount of fiberfill on the shovel to look like snow. Attach a piece of sticky-back magnet to the back of the shovel.

You might want to try making a shovel magnet from a different-colored plastic plate.

Snowman Zipper-Pull

Here is what you need:

orange and black felt scraps

empty white plastic bottle such as dish soap comes in

tiny hole punch

red yarn scrap

black permanent marker

paper clip

white craft glue

ballpoint pen

scissors

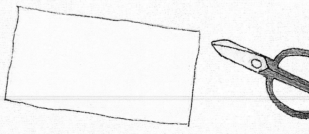

WHEN IT IS COLD OUTSIDE WE WEAR WARM, HEAVY COATS.

Here is what you do:

1. Use scissors to cut a flat piece from the side of the plastic bottle.

2. Use the pen to sketch the outline of a small snowman on the plastic.

3. Cut out the snowman shape.

4. Use the hole punch to punch a tiny hole in the top of the snowman shape.

5. Slide a paper clip through the hole so that the snowman can be attached to a zipper.

6. Cut a tiny hat for the snowman from the black felt scrap. Glue the hat to the head of the snowman.

7. Cut a tiny carrot nose from the orange felt scrap. Glue the nose to the head of the snowman.

8. Use the black marker to give the snowman eyes, a smile, and some buttons.

9. Tie a piece of red yarn around the neck of the snowman for a scarf.

Hang the little snowman off the zipper of your warm winter jacket or coat and go outside to play in the snow. Snowmen love cold weather.

Melting Snowman

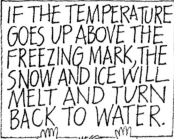

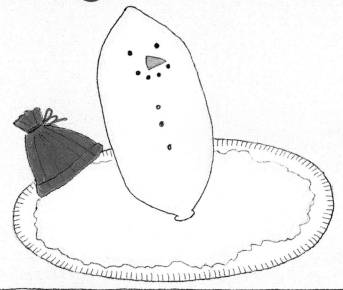

Here is what you need:

long, white airship-type balloon

colorful adult sock with stretchy cuff

scissors

thin craft ribbon

permanent markers

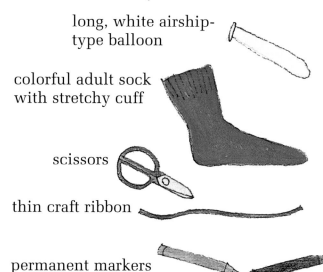

paper plate

white craft glue

large paper clip

fiberfill

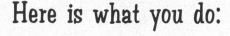

Here is what you do:

1. Poke a small hole through the center of the paper plate.

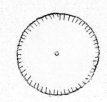

2. Glue fiberfill all over the eating side of the plate to look like snow. Do not block the hole in the center of the plate.

3. Push the neck of the balloon down through the snow-covered plate.

4. Blow up the balloon. Secure the air in the balloon by sliding the paper clip over the neck of the balloon, then wrapping the neck around the paper clip and sliding it through the clip again.

5. Use the markers to give the balloon snowman a face and buttons.

6. Cut the cuff from the sock to make a hat for the snowman.

7. Tie one end of the cuff shut with a piece of ribbon.

8. Slide the hat over the top of the balloon.

To "melt" the snowman, remove the paper clip and slowly release the air from the balloon. You might want to make the Sun Puppet on page 22 to shine on the snowman as it melts.

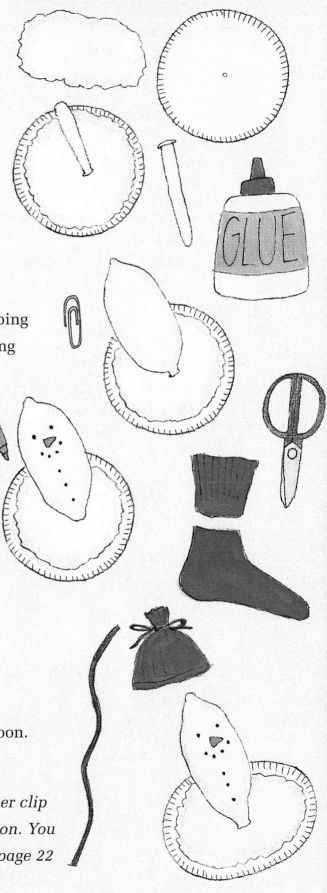

About the Author and Artist

Thirty years as a teacher and director of nursery school programs have given Kathy Ross extensive experience in guiding young children through crafts projects. Among the more than forty craft books she has written are **Crafts For All Seasons, More of the Best Holiday Crafts Ever, The Storytime Craft Book,** and the **All New Holiday Crafts for Kids** series. You can find out more about Kathy's books by visiting her at www.Kathyross.com

Jan Barger, originally from Little Rock, Arkansas, now lives in Plumpton, East Sussex, England with her husband and their cocker spaniel, Tosca. She has written and illustrated a number of children's books and is known for her gentle humor and warm, friendly characters. She also designs greeting cards, sings with the Brighton Festival Chorus and plays piccolo with the Sinfonia of Arun.

Together, Kathy and Jan have written and illustrated **Crafts for Kids Who Are Learning about Community Workers** as well as the **Learning is Fun** series.